4·99

ents

Acknowledgements

The publishers would like to thank Wilson for their photographic contribution to this book.

Photographs on inside front cover, inside back cover and pages 6 and 15 courtesy of Sporting Pictures. All other photographs courtesy of Allsport UK Ltd.

Thanks to Alasdair Barr, PGA Swing Tutor.

Illustrations by Margaret Jones.

Note Throughout the book players, scorers and markers are referred to individually as 'he'. This should, of course, be taken to mean 'he or she' where appropriate. Similarly, the instructions throughout the text are geared towards right-handed players and left-handers should simply reverse these instructions.

D0260479

Introduction

This book is essentially a guide to the game of golf and is not meant to be a complete reference.

The official Rules of Golf are governed by the Royal and Ancient Golf Club of St. Andrews. This book is not meant to be a substitute for the official publication but should be read in conjunction with it. The rules governing situations described in this book are shown in brackets at the end of each section.

The Rules of Golf are published by Royal Insurance and are available free of charge from Royal Insurance (UK) Ltd, PO Liverpool

The game

The Game of Golf consists of playing a ball from the teeing ground into the hole by successive strokes in accordance with the rules. (Rule 1)

A full-sized course consists of 18 holes: usually four 'short' holes, which measure up to 250 yds (229 m) from tee to green and can be covered by one full stroke; and 14 longer holes, from 250 to 500 yds (229–457 m) or more in length, and requiring two or three full strokes from tee to green. One round of the course is the usual length of a match, but in some competitions two or more rounds are played. One round occupies about three hours.

The space between tee and green at the long holes is occupied by mown turf called the 'fairway', and on either side of the fairway are rough grass, trees, bushes, etc. There are also 'hazards' of various kinds, mainly sand bunkers but occasionally streams, ditches, and ponds. The 'green' is a closely mown surface for putting and the 'hole' is sunk in the green and marked with a flag. (*See* fig. 1.)

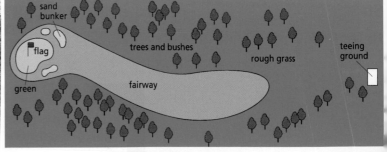

2

Etiquette

In addition to the rules, the game also has a code of etiquette, which should be observed by all golfers and studied with particular care by beginners. Adherence to these rules of behaviour helps to make the game more enjoyable for everyone. The rules of etiquette are quoted in full on pages 40–1, but can be summarised as follows.

The Ten Commandments of etiquette

1 Always play without undue delay. If your match has 'lost' one complete hole always ask the match behind to 'play through', and stand well to the side as they do so. The same applies if your match should lose a ball.

2 Do not play a stroke until the match in front is out of range. Should the ball go anywhere near a fellow player a warning cry of 'Fore!' is *always* used.

3 Always stand well clear of the person making a stroke, for your own safety and so as not to distract the

player by obscuring his vision. Stand still and quiet, ideally facing the player.

4 'Divots' – the grass removed when playing an iron shot – should always be replaced. Holes and footmarks in sand traps – or 'bunkers' – must be smoothed out with the rake provided or with the head of an iron club.

5 Bags must not be laid on the green because they may cause damage.

6 Trollies should be left well to the side of the green so as not to damage the surrounds.

7 The first player to hole out on the putting green should retrieve the flag in readiness to replace it in the cup when the last player has holed out.

8 Score cards should be marked on the next tee and not on the putting green.

9 In the absence of special rules, two-ball matches have precedence over three- and four-ball matches. A single player playing should give way to a match of any kind.

10 Do not move, talk, stand too close to or directly behind the player when a stroke is being played.

Clubs

Two rules prohibit the use of any club or ball which does not conform to clearly defined specifications and fundamental principles of design. Clubs must have all the various parts fixed and not capable of adjustment. Concave faces are banned, as are those having markings which do not satisfy the current requirements or are modified for the purpose of unduly influencing the movement of the ball.

The grip on the shaft may not have a channel or furrow or be moulded to the hands, and the shaft itself must be fixed to the heel of the club-head, except in the case of a putter. The shaft of a putter may be fixed at any point in the head, but must be straight and must diverge from the vertical by at least 10° from a point not more than 5 in (13 cm) above the sole.

An 'iron' club is one with a head which is usually relatively narrow from face to back, and is normally made of steel. A 'wood' club is one with a head relatively broad from face to back, and is usually made of wood, plastic, or a light metal. (*Rule 4*)

The numbers on the iron clubs indicate the distances for which the clubs are designed. The higher the number of the club, the higher the ball will fly, the less time it spends going forwards, and the less the distance it travels. Therefore, the low numbers are used for long shots, and the high numbers for short shots.

To give an indication of this principle, there follows a table showing approximate distances that can be achieved regularly with different clubs.

3-wood: 200 yds+ (180 m+)
4-iron: 170–180 yds (155–165 m)
6-iron: 150–160 yds (135–145 m)
8-iron: 130–140 yds (120–130 m)
wedge: 100–120 yds (90–110 m)

Choosing clubs

The maximum number of clubs a golfer is allowed to carry is 14, but the beginner can start quite happily with a half-set. This need not be expensive, indeed a second-hand set is perfectly adequate at this stage.

Whether you choose a new or second-hand set, the important factor is that the clubs should fit you and not vice versa. It is therefore essential to seek the advice of a PGA professional. His services are available to everyone, whether members of a golf club or not. He will be able to advise you on the correct clubs and make any adjustments that are necessary.

In the proposed half-set you will need at least four irons. Choose alternate odd or even numbers, but it is probably best to start at the 4-iron because clubs with little loft are more difficult to use. You may choose, say, a 4-iron, a 6-iron, an 8-iron and a wedge (some sets refer to the wedge as a 10-iron, but the degree of loft is exactly the same). In addition, choose a wooden club, ideally a 3-wood which can double as a club to drive with and a fairway wood. Finally, you will need to choose a putter. There are literally thousands of different styles of putter so how does the beginner go about choosing one that will be suitable? A PGA professional will accompany you on to the putting green and allow you to try different styles, weights and club lie. With his help and in a process of elimination you will arrive at the putter of your choice.

Buying clubs

When buying golf clubs there are three very important factors to be taken into account: shaft flex, lie of the club, grip thickness.

Shaft flex

Shaft flex can be broken down into four categories – stiff, regular, 'A' and women's. To denote shaft flex, manufacturers place the appropriate symbol on a label around the club shaft.

'Stiff' – marked 'S' – is suited to the player with strong hands and an aggressive swing because he does not require any 'help' from the shaft (i.e. his club-head speed is sufficiently fast). 'Regular' – marked 'R' – is suitable for the average player. The 'A' shaft is suited to the older golfer: it is slightly softer and will provide a little more club-head speed as the 'whippiness' (shaft flex) unwinds through the ball. The women's shaft (marked 'L' for 'Ladies') is even softer than the 'A' shaft and is suited to women and children because they do not generate a great deal of club-head speed.

Lie of the club

The lie of the club is the angle at which the shaft extends from the head when the sole (bottom) of the club is resting on the grass. It is vital to return the club-face to the ball at impact exactly as it was placed behind the ball before the swing. If the toe of the club is off the ground, the club-face will close because the heel strikes the ground first. Alternatively, if the heel is off the ground, the club-face will open as the toe catches the ground.

There is a popular misconception that taller players need longer than standard clubs, and that shorter players require shorter shafts. The length of the club has nothing whatsoever to do with the height of the golfer. Most of our bodies are in proportion, i.e. tall people have long arms, etc. Buying a set of clubs on the basis of your height will ruin your game before it has barely started.

The determining factor is how far your clenched fist hangs from the ground: this is the distance that the club shaft has to cover to meet your hand.

Grip thickness

It is important that your clubs are fitted with the right size of grip. If the grip is too thick, the club will be held too much in the palm of the hands and this will reduce the much needed wrist action required in the swing. Conversely, the grip that is too thin will allow the club to be gripped too much in the fingers and the wrist action will be excessive. Over-active wrists often cause 'hooking': a lack of wrist action often causes 'slicing'. The size of a player's hand is the guide to the correct thickness: a PGA professional will know exactly how to advise you.

Grips are made of two basic materials – leather and rubber. The choice between the two is a matter of personal preference, although as leather has become very expensive the rubber grip is much more common and considerably easier to maintain. If they become shiny or slippery, rubber grips can be given a thorough scrub with a nail-brush and soapy water. This will remove the dirt and perspiration that everyday play will cause to accumu-late on the grip: the little brown cork specks visible in the rubber absorb soap, giving the grip a nice tacky feel. If this treatment does not have much effect, have some new grips fitted. Again, a PGA professional is there to help.

The ball

The weight of the ball may not be greater than 1.62 oz (45.9 g) and the size not less than 1.68 in (42.7 mm) in diameter. There is also a velocity/compression standard and only balls on the approved lists of conforming balls of the R. and A. and the United States Golf Association are legal. (*Rule 5*)

There are basically three types of golf ball in production:

• two-piece or solid ball
• three-piece ball
• wound ball.

The two-piece ball is well suited to the beginner since it is very durable (cut proof) and travels a greater distance because the centre is already compressed.

The three-piece ball is slightly softer but has a surlyn (man-made) cover. Because it is softer it does not travel quite as far as the two-piece; as a result it stops more quickly on the greens. With the surlyn cover it is also very durable.

The wound ball is used by the low-handicap player and the tournament professional. This ball has a very soft cover made from balata (a natural material) and it is conducive to generating spin on landing, which makes it much easier to control. The softer cover, however, marks more easily from mis-hits.

Equipment checklist

The following is a checklist of equipment that a golfer will need out on the course:

- clubs (maximum 14)
- bag (and trolley/cart if necessary)
- balls
- tees
- glove (optional, though recommended)
- ball markers
- pitch repairer
- head covers (to keep club-heads clean and dry)
- towel (especially to keep club shafts dry)
- water-proof clothing
- umbrella
- golf shoes (preferably spiked)
- sun visor (optional, though useful).

Address

A player has 'addressed the ball' when he has taken his stance and grounded his club (or, in a hazard, taken his stance).

A player's address or 'set-up' is vital because it pre-determines the swing movement and presents the club-head at impact. Most swing errors stem from a faulty address position.

At the address, the feet should be approximately as far apart as the width of your shoulders, with the weight evenly distributed; the toes should be pointed outwards slightly and the knees flexed inwards a little. The left arm, wrist and club should be almost in a straight line, with hands slightly ahead of the club-head. The body should not be too crouched nor too upright, but just between the two.

If the ball moves after address it must be replaced, not played as it lays.

In order to achieve the correct position consistently a sequence is adhered to: grip, stance and ball placement.

Grip

The most common way of gripping a club is known as the 'Vardon' (or 'over-lapping') grip, named after its originator Harry Vardon. (*See* fig. 2.) The left hand is fitted first by placing the grip of the club through the middle joint of the index finger, across the palm, about $^{1}/_{2}$–$^{3}/_{4}$ in (12–20 mm) above the end of the small finger. The hand is then closed round the handle and two or three knuckles should be visible on the back of the left hand, dependent on the size of the player's hand. A 'V' will have been formed between the index finger and the thumb, and this 'V' will point mid-way between the player's right shoulder and chin, again depending on the size of the player's hands.

The right hand is fitted by positioning the grip on the middle joint of the index finger diagonally across the palm so the club passes along the end of the small finger. The hand is closed on to the grip and the 'V' will point in the same direction as that on the left hand. This will mean that the hands have been 'married' and will work together as a unit. The small finger is then fitted so it overlaps the index finger of the left hand.

There are two alternatives to this grip (*see* pages 12–13).

▶   *Fig. 2 Vardon grip: first fit the left hand by placing the grip of the club through the middle joint of the index finger, across the palm, about $^{1}/_{2}$–$^{3}/_{4}$ in (12–20 mm) above the end of the small finger. Close the hand around the handle so that two or three knuckles are visible. The 'V' formed between the index finger and the thumb must point mid-way between your right shoulder and your chin*

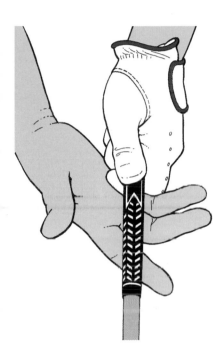

▲ *Fit the right hand by positioning the grip on the middle joint of the index finger diagonally across the palm so the club passes along the end of the small finger*

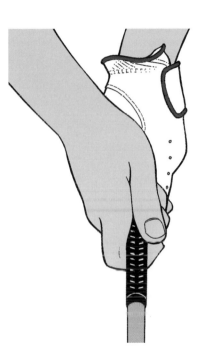

▲ *Close the right hand on to the grip and the 'V' will point in the same direction as that on the left hand*

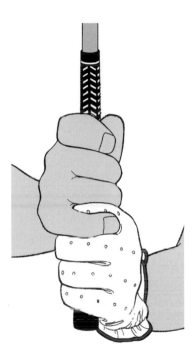

▲ *The small finger on the right hand is fitted so it overlaps the index finger of the left hand*

11

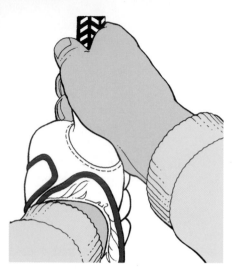

▲ *Vardon grip (cont.) The 'V' shapes point mid-way between the right shoulder and the chin, depending on the size of your hands*

▶ *Fig. 3 Interlocking grip: position the club in the hands in exactly the same way as for the Vardon grip . . .*

Interlocking grip

The position of the club in the hands is exactly the same as has been described for the Vardon grip. However, the left index finger and the right small finger are intertwined. (*See* fig. 3.) This grip is used by players with small hands.

▼ *. . . but in this grip the left index finger and the right small finger are intertwined*

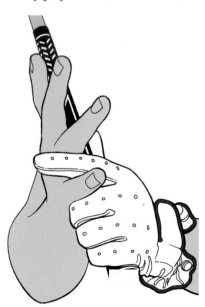

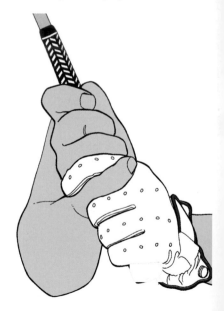

Two-handed or 'baseball' grip

Here, all fingers of the hands are placed on the grip. (See fig. 4.) This grip is favoured by golfers with short fingers, particularly women and juniors, but it is not to be recommended as an ideal because the hands remain totally separated when they ought to be united.

If your hands or fingers are small, it is advisable to have a PGA professional fit thinner grips to your clubs.

Common grip faults

In what is known as a 'strong' grip (see fig. 5), the hands are placed on the club too far to the player's right. The 'V' shapes formed by the thumb and index finger of each hand point to the right of the right shoulder. The hands will always try to return to the correct position: the result is the club-face will close at impact, usually causing 'hooked' shots to the left.

With a 'weak' grip (see fig. 6), the hands on the club are turned too far to the player's left. The 'V' shape of each hand points to the left of the chin. Consequently the player will find it extremely difficult to square the club-face at impact and the ball will tend to be 'sliced' to the right of the target.

▶ *Fig. 5 (top) A 'strong' grip*

▶ *Fig. 6 (bottom) A 'weak' grip*

◀ *Fig. 4 Two-handed/'baseball' grip: all the fingers of both hands are placed on the grip*

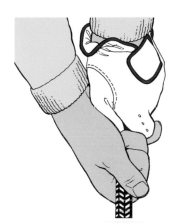

Stance

The stance is adopted with two objectives in mind: to support the player during the swing, and to align the player to the target.

Since the widest part of the body is the area across the shoulders, the player will need a firm base to support this area. The feet on a full shot, therefore, should be approximately shoulder width apart.

As a club's length shortens, so the stance will narrow, because body movement decreases and the narrower stance will make it easier to maintain control.

When the stance is adopted, an imaginary line drawn through the toes should run parallel to the line from the ball to the actual target. A useful analogy here is of standing on a railway track, the club-head on one rail and the toes on the other. (See fig. 7.) With the feet, hips and shoulders in line, this position is referred to as a 'square' stance.

▲ *Fig. 7 To adopt a 'square' stance, imagine standing on a railway track with the club-head on one rail and the toes on the other*

Closed stance

In a 'closed' stance the feet, hips and shoulders point to the right of the target line. (*See* fig. 8.) This type of stance will encourage the ball to start to the right of the target and spin to the left in flight. If the ball finishes on the target line this shot is called a 'draw'. If, however, it moves further to the left it is referred to as a 'hook'. (*See* fig. 10.)

▲ *Fig. 8 A 'closed' stance is characterised by the feet, hips and shoulders pointing to the right of the target line*

14

Open stance

In an 'open' stance the feet, hips and shoulders aim to the left of the target line. (*See* fig. 9.) As a result the ball will be encouraged to start to the left of the target, and spin to the right. If the ball finishes on the target line this shot is called a 'fade'. If, however, it moves uncontrollably to the right it is referred to as a 'slice'. (*See* fig. 10.)

All these effects are created by swing paths that create spin on the ball; the swing path is controlled by the alignment of the player's feet, hips and shoulders.

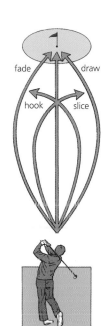

▲ *Fig. 10 The alignment of a player's feet, hips and shoulders controls his swing path, which in turn can create these effects on the ball's flight*

◄ *Fig. 9 An 'open' stance is characterised by the feet, hips and shoulders pointing to the left of the target line*

Ball placement

Ball placement controls the effect on the ball.

Short and medium iron shots are hit with back-spin in order to make the ball stop quickly when it lands on the green. The ball is placed in the centre of the stance so that it is hit slightly on the downswing. (*See* fig. 11.)

With longer irons the ball is played from slightly closer to the left shoe; with wooden or metal-headed clubs it is positioned approximately in line with the left heel. (*See* fig. 11.) Thus the ball is hit slightly on the upswing, reducing back-spin to a minimum and helping to create distance.

To position the ball, place the feet completely together. Move the left foot into position, then take the right foot forwards to complement this and to achieve a shoulder width stance. At all times keep the imaginary line through the toes pointing at the target.

The distance the player should stand from the ball should be dictated by the length of the shaft of the club being used. The longer the club's shaft, the further away your distance from the ball. (*See* fig. 11.) Personal comfort is the other important factor: too far away will restrict movement; too close will cause loss of balance and control.

▶ *Fig. 11 Ball placement: the distance a player should stand from the ball should be dictated by the length of the shaft of the club being used. With short and medium iron clubs, place the ball in the centre of the stance. With longer irons, place it slightly closer to the left shoe. With wooden clubs, place it approximately in line with the left heel*

The swing

Making the stroke

A 'stroke' is the forward movement of the club made with the intention of fairly striking at and moving the ball.

The mechanics of the golf swing consist of swinging the club backwards and upwards from the address position to a position above and behind the head from which a downward and forward blow can be aimed at the ball.

To hit a golf ball successfully your whole body must be committed to the swing. All of its moving parts have one aim – to allow the club to swing. Regardless of which club is being used, there is only one swing.

Consider the parts of your anatomy that combine to allow the swing to function as a free-moving unit. The body can be divided into two areas: the upper body (from the waist up), to include the arms and shoulders; and the lower body – the hips, legs and feet.

The swinging effect will come from your upper body; the real source of power is the lower body.

At this stage it is important to realise that the successful golf shot requires two elements – direction and power. It is that simple. If you work on the movements that will permit this to happen, you will have a useful understanding of how to move a club in the correct fashion, and a good chance of being consistent too.

The waggle

As a preliminary to the swing the player should instigate what is called the 'waggle'. This is a gentle movement back and forth with the club-head, hands and wrists, designed to ease the tension of the set-up and encourage a rhythmic start to the back-swing.

17

The half-swing

For the process of building a swing, start with the half-swing; that is, taking the club back to waist level on both the back-swing and the follow-through. (*See* fig. 12.)

Before moving the club there is a fundamental concept to consider. As has been stated earlier, the target line is an imaginary line that runs from the ball to the target. The area to the player's side of the line is called 'inside'. The area to the other side (to the right of the target line as viewed from behind), is called 'outside' the line.

To build the swing start with a medium-iron, say a 6- or 7-iron. These clubs are the link between the long and the short irons. They are relatively easy to control and at the same time allow the pupil to hit the ball far enough for him to be able to analyse the ball's flight path.

▶ *Fig. 12 The half-swing*

The set-up: an attempt to pre-set the impact position. The left hand, arm and shaft form a continuous line. The club is, therefore, an extension of the arm and the two work together. The body is nicely relaxed, ready for physical activity

At waist level the shoulder is following the arm and the weight is transferring on to the right leg, creating the correct co-ordination

Impact: we have all but returned to the set-up position. The only difference is that the momentum of the swing has carried the legs and feet forwards towards the target. The arm-shaft relationship is identical

This position is a mirror image of the back-swing. The two halves of the swing belong to each other . . . balance is the result

18

One-piece take-away

The first movement of the back-swing (or 'take-away') is to move the club back along the target line, keeping it as low to the ground as possible for the first 12 in (30 cm); even further for longer clubs.

By extending the left hand and arm back to waist level, the left shoulder must follow and the club will naturally swing inside the line.

At waist level the club-face will now appear to point off to the right. In fact, it is still square to the target and this can be checked in two ways. Firstly, the leading edge of the club-face will still be at right angles to the shoulders, and the knuckles visible on the back of the left hand will still be the same as in the set-up. Secondly, due to the extension back from the ball, you will feel the weight transferring to the right side. This is not a conscious action, but a responsive one. The right knee remains comfortably flexed as in the set-up. All parts of the body are encouraged to work together.

The first 18–24 in (45–60 cm) is the most important phase of the golf swing. Do your best to ensure that the club-face remains square to the target, and see that the big muscles of the shoulders and legs are encouraged to become involved.

The forward swing commences with the lateral movement of the hips and legs. The left heel, which will have cleared the ground on the back-swing (although only marginally because a half-swing was made), will then return to the ground. There cannot be a lateral shift if the left heel remains off the ground. The hands and arms will then swing through to waist level, and your body weight will now be on the left shoe. Already co-ordination has been created as both club and player are moving in the same direction at the same time. During this half-swing no conscious effort should be made to hit the ball. You should feel that contact is made because the ball happens to be in the way of the path of the club-head.

Once you have experienced this back-and-forward movement, and all the responsive actions, you are ready to progress on to the full swing. (*See* fig. 13.)

The full swing

The back-swing

Having invited the left shoulder into the swing by means of extension, the back-swing is completed by turning the left shoulder through approximately 90°. You should be aware of turning the left shoulder between your eyes and the ball. Your body weight will transfer even further on to the right side and you will feel your whole body weight over your right hip, knee and ankle. As the hips will have turned through only 45°, there will be a feeling of tension around the hip muscles. This means that your upper body has been 'wound up' against your lower body; when this tension is released, you have created the ability to hit the ball powerfully.

At the top of the swing the left arm should be *comfortably* straight, not held deliberately straight because this is really physically impossible.

The wrist action (or wrist 'cock') that will occur on the back-swing is caused by the weight of the club and

Fig. 13 The full swing

Same set-up as for the half-swing

Note the wide take-away inviting the large muscles of the shoulders and legs into the shot

The back-swing is completed by the 90° turn of the shoulders. This creates a winding-up effect between the upper and lower body. The body weight is now almost totally on the right side . . . but the right leg is still flexed. The left arm is held comfortably straight

The tension created around the hips in the previous position is now released. The weight transfers, at speed, on to the left side

The moment of impact. The head is held in a central position as the hands, arms and club-head are released through to the target. No attempt to 'hit at' the ball is made. Allow the club-head to make contact with the ball merely because it happens to be in the way of the path of the club-head

Full extension of the arms and a continuing of weight transference to the left. No attempt is made to 'keep the head down' because this has a restricting effect on the follow-through

The completed follow-through . . . with the hands in a nice high position . . . the body weight fully committed to the left side . . . and the upper body facing the target

20

the momentum of the swing. This wrist cock is *never* a conscious action. It will break the line of the swing if you try to perform it as a deliberate movement.

At the top of the back-swing the line along the club shaft will again be parallel to the ball-to-target line. You should feel that your body has been 'wound up' or coiled like a spring; this provides the means with which to hit the ball. If it is possible to hold this position for any length of time, nothing has been created. When you instinctively relax this tension at speed, the spring is released.

The muscles of the shoulders and legs are now totally committed. It is these muscles that dictate the speed and rhythm of the swing, because they take longer to move than the smaller muscles in the hands and wrists. By being conscious of moving the large muscles in your shoulders in the second half of the back-swing, you prevent the swing from becoming too quick – a big problem when you experience pressure in competitive situations.

The down-swing

You are now fully prepared to strike the ball and follow through. From the top of the back-swing the tension that you create will be released instinctively and your body weight can transfer completely to your left side. As the left heel clears the ground on the back-swing you create a space to move back into as it returns to the ground.

The forward drive of the legs which creates the power will totally commit your body weight to the left leg and shoe; you will be almost able to lift your right foot off the ground.

The follow-through and finish of the swing are *reactions* to the back-swing rather than consciously adopted positions. The follow-through is the product of a good swing, *not vice versa*.

The 'release' is a result of all the other movements of the correct swing. It is not a conscious motion made with the hands. It is a movement that takes place *after* the ball has been struck, and not before. Allow the hands and arms to swing through freely. They will finish high around the head. The upper body will point at the target.

The legs

Remember that the real power stems from the legs, not the hands. (Because the legs respond instinctively, it is tempting to feel that they are inactive. Nothing could be further from the truth.) The most useful analogy is that of a boxer throwing a punch. If he keeps his feet flat on the ground, of course, he could still hit his opponent, but the punch wouldn't do a great deal of damage. However, if he allows his body weight to move in the same direction as his fist, then all his movements are co-ordinated and his body weight reinforces his fist and extra power is generated. For the golfer, substitute 'club-head' for 'fist'.

The head

The frequently heard advice of 'Keep your head down' is one of the golfing myths. The head should be held steady throughout the back-swing and for most of the follow-through. However, as the momentum of the swing takes the club-head through to approximately waist level, the head should be allowed to rise in order that the player can see where the ball has gone. The problem with keeping the head down is that this breeds a tendency to bury the chin in the chest, clamping the head into a fixed position.

Swing plane

There is one swing for all clubs. All the different shots that are required and the distances that have to be achieved are the responsibilities of the clubs themselves. However, the beginner may notice when watching other people playing that different clubs appear to swing on different angles around the body. For example, the swing for the shorter irons may appear to be more upright than that for the longer irons and wooden clubs. This is due entirely to the length of the shaft, and the angle between the shaft and the ground.

The angle that the club travels around the body is referred to as the 'swing plane'. Though in terms of the swing the swing plane is extremely important, happily the plane is virtually self-finding. It is decided by the angle of the individual's spine, which in turn is decided by his height and the length of the club shaft.

The striking sensation when hitting with a wooden club is that of a sweeping action. With the iron clubs, because of the divot taken (slight with the long irons, bigger with the shorter irons), it is more of a *punching* action. This is not a conscious act by the player, but a result of the ball position and the other factors previously discussed.

As you stand closer for the shorter clubs, the spinal angle will be more severe; therefore the swing will be more upright. With a longer shaft, the straighter spine will mean the shoulder turn is flattened. So while you may feel the swing is slightly different initially, the basic movement of the upper and lower body is unchanged.

The short game

The short game falls into two categories: chipping and pitching. A chip shot is used when a player is situated close to the putting surface but is unable to putt the ball. Pitching is a restricted version of the full swing, and is used when a player is too far from the green to chip.

23

Chipping

Many of the techniques which apply to putting also apply to chipping as the strokes involved are very similar.

The idea of the chip shot is to play the ball from where it lies and fly it to the nearest available flat area of the green, letting it run out on the nicely prepared surface to the hole. By landing the ball first bounce on the green it eliminates the unpredictable bounce that could result from landing the ball on the fairway or fringe grass.

Club selection is a vitally important part of being a successful 'chipper'. The basic rule is that if you can't putt the ball, use a 7-iron, and if that is not suitable then use a wedge. The choice of club is thus determined by the situation in which the player finds himself.

The easiest method of judging distance is to keep the ball as close to the ground as possible. If a player applies 10 yards worth of effort to a putting stroke, the ball will travel 10 yards because it spends its whole journey going forwards. The same strength applied to a 7-iron, for example, with its 36° of loft, will send the ball only about 7–8 yards, as the club will use some of the energy in the shot to make the ball rise. Therefore, to achieve a distance of 10 yards, a little more effort has to be applied, so hand/eye co-ordination becomes a little more important.

If the shot were to be played with a wedge, even more effort would have to be applied as the club has a higher degree of loft.

The chip shot is played using a standard hold, although the hands can be positioned towards the bottom of the grip, the shorter shaft being easier to control. A conscious effort should be made to hold the club lightly as this will increase club-head 'feel'.

The width of the stance can be reduced as there is little or no body movement to this shot, so a stable base is not essential for the level of effort required.

The alignment of the body is, as always, parallel to the target line, although a little more bodyweight can be positioned on the left side. By positioning the ball in the centre of the stance, the hands will be encouraged to stay ahead of the ball.

The swing is the same as the putting stroke. It is a pendulum-style swing with passive wrists and the weight remaining as at the set-up. Backswing and forward swing should be of similar length. The length of the backswing controls the distance the ball will travel, and an even-paced follow through will encourage good direction.

A general indication of distance would be as follows:

7-iron	25% flight, 75% bounce and roll
wedge	50% flight, 50% bounce and roll

Pitching

The basic principle of pitching is that by using a restricted swing, the club will propel the ball less than the distance achieved by a full swing.

The length of the back-swing will determine the distance the ball travels. This can be controlled from the set-up position. By narrowing the width of the stance, the back-swing will automatically be reduced in length, however the feet should never be less than 2–3 inches apart as a narrower stance would be too unsympathetic to the width of the shoulder. If there is still too much back-swing, the player should move the hands down the shaft, thus automatically reducing the arc of the swing still further.

The important factor at the set-up is that the position adopted is consistent with the length of the back-swing required.

As with the chip, the strength of the grip should be lighter than normal. The alignment should be as for a full shot, with the weight favoured to the left side on a 60/40 ratio.

The swing should feel like a mini-version of the full shot, the only difference being that the power in the leg and shoulder muscles has been reduced.

As the wedge is one of the shortest clubs, and the weight is favouring the left side, the wrists will automatically and naturally become involved earlier and there is therefore no need for the player to consciously intervene.

Once the length of the back-swing has been restricted, the club-head is released freely through the ball. The weight will transfer almost fully to the left side, and the follow-through should be of similar length to the back-swing.

No attempt should be made to help the ball into the air. Trust the loft of the club to do this for you.

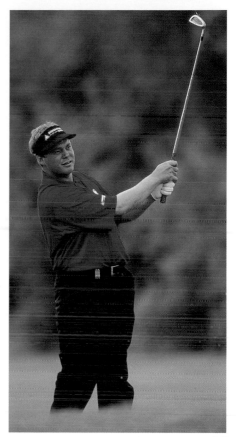

Putting

Putting is the most precise part of the game and arguably the most important, for strokes can be saved by good putting and wasted by bad putting. The normal average allowance is two putts per green, but a golfer who is putting well usually beats this average.

Technique

Putting *style* counts for nothing: if it works then it's right! For every player there is a different and personal style.

The guideline here, above all else, is to feel comfortable and balanced. The width of stance and the position of the feet are relatively unimportant. Because the grip on the club has a flat front, there has to be an adjustment to the way in which it is held. Both thumbs are therefore positioned straight down the front of the handle. This will mean that the back of the left hand and the palm of the right will be facing the target, as will the blade of the putter, so the two hands are working together, and the club is held lightly.

The basic principle of the putting stroke is to create a pendulum effect. The length of the back-swing governs the length of the putt, and the follow-through controls direction. As it is a pendulum motion the follow-through, at worst, must be the same length as the back-swing. However, you can follow through almost as far as you wish without affecting the distance that the ball travels.

The ball is not 'hit' as such because this will result in loss of control. It should be much more of a stroking motion: the putter-head should make passive contact with the ball. During the stroke the head of the putter should be kept as close to the ground as possible, encouraging it to swing on a straight line to and from the target.

Sweet spot

To find the correct place to position the ball on the blade of the putter we need to know the location of the 'sweet spot' (or 'balanced point') on the head. If the ball is not struck on the sweet spot, but on either the toe or the heel of the putter-head, the club will be twisted at impact. This will mean that the ball will be struck out of line and will not run 'true', i.e. end over end.

The sweet spot is found by holding the grip end of the putter lightly in the thumb and forefinger at shoulder level; then with the third finger of the right hand gently tap the face of the putter in different places. On one spot the head will swing on a true line. This is the sweet spot or 'striking point'. Most modern-day putters do in fact have a line on the top edge of the head to indicate this position, but it is worth checking nonetheless.

Reading the green

'Reading the green' is the expression used to denote the task of finding the line that the ball should be set out on to allow for the green's contours (the 'borrow'). It essentially consists of the player's own judgement in trying to assess the severity of the slope. Once you have assessed the slope, choose a spot on the green a few inches in front of the ball and aim at that mark. This, in effect, makes every putt straight.

Remember that if the line to the hole is downhill, the ball will roll down the slope quickly and any 'borrow' will affect its path noticeably. An over-hit downhill putt will invariably leave a relatively easier uphill putt to follow.

Uphill putts should be struck more firmly in order to get the ball up the slope to the hole. The effect of 'borrow' will be less, but remember that an over-hit uphill putt will invariably leave a tricky downhill putt to follow.

It is vital that a practice swing is made before every putt; this will encourage hand-eye co-ordination for the length of putt to be executed.

Keeping score

Score cards like that shown on page 29 are used for marking a competitor's score in a Medal, Stableford or Match Play Against Par (Bogey) competition. In Medal play the competitor's full handicap is deducted from his total score. In Stableford competitions it is usual that $7/8$ of the handicap is taken and in Match Play Against Par (Bogey) competitions $3/4$ of the handicap is taken. In matches, the player with the higher handicap receives $3/4$ of the difference between his handicap and that of his opponent.

A score card imparts a great deal of useful information to the golfer. Each hole is numbered (and named in this instance). Two distance measurements are given to indicate the length of each hole, the first from the tournament (white) tees and the second from the non-tournament (yellow) tees. Then comes the par for each hole. In red is the stroke index for each hole, an indication of where handicap strokes are taken in Match Play Against Par (Bogey) or Stableford competitions. For example, a player having 12 strokes takes one at the 10th hole (numbered 12) and one each at all other holes having a stroke index less than 12 (i.e. the 2nd, 3rd, 4th, 5th, 7th, 8th, 12th, 14th, 15th, 16th and 18th). A player having only three strokes takes them at the 4th, 5th and 16th holes.

The player's score is in strokes. This is always given as the gross score – the number of strokes actually played – and inserted by the marker. Handicap calculations are made afterwards.

The final column of each hole shows the results of each hole compared with par. If the player's net score for the hole (after deducting any handicap stroke) is less than the par score he marks '+', indicating a win. If the score is the same the Committee marks '0', indicating a halved hole. If the score is higher than par the Committee marks '–', indicating a loss.

Both the player and marker *must* sign the card before it is handed in.

COMPETITION								DATE		TIME		Handicap		Strokes Received	

Player A									Please indicate which tee used.						
Player B									PAR 72 S.S.S. 71	PAR 72 S.S.S. 69					

Hole	Markers Score	Name	White Yards	Yellow Yards	Par	Stroke index	Score A	Score B	W= + L= − H= 0 points	Hole	Markers Score	Name	White Yards	Yellow Yards	Par	Stroke index	Score A	Score B	W= + L= − H= 0 points
1		Elizabeth 1	330	318	4	13				10		Icehouse	550	510	5	12			
2		Paine	191	151	3	7				11		Walker	493	476	5	16			
3		Templehill	491	471	5	9				12		Cipriani	353	324	4	4			
4		Lodgehill	465	422	4	3				13		Enzo	342	328	4	18			
5		Joseph Woods	471	443	4	1				14		Caroline Lamb	221	194	3	8			
6		Byron	174	160	3	15				15		Four Gates	384	363	4	6			
7		Crackendell	312	302	4	5				16		Waterfall	422	402	4	2			
8		Cats Gallows	303	363	4	11				17		Avenue	330	305	4	14			
9		Prince Regent	148	132	3	17				18		Broadwater	509	484	5	10			
	OUT		2965	2762	34						IN		3604	3386	38				
											OUT		2965	2762	34				
											TOTAL		6569	6148	72				

HANDICAP

NETT

Markers Signature...

Players Signature...

Holes Won...........

Holes Lost...........

Result.................

STABLEFORD POINTS OR PAR RESULT

▲ *Fig. 14 A typical score card (courtesy of Brocket Hall Golf Club, Welwyn, Herts)*

Rules of the game

Number of clubs allowed

A player cannot start a round with more than 14 clubs. He may replace a club which becomes unfit for use during the course of play, as long as he does not unduly delay play. *(Rule 6–7)*

A complete set of 14 clubs can be obtained, consisting usually of either four woods, nine irons and a putter; or three woods, ten irons and a putter, depending on the individual preference of the player.

The length of a golf club varies from roughly 42 in (107 cm) for a driver to 35 in (89 cm) for a short iron or putter, diminishing at half-inch (1.3 cm) intervals. As the club diminishes in length, so the club face increases in weight and angle of loft, e.g. the driver at 42 in (107 cm) has an angle of loft on its face of 11°, the 5-iron at 38 in (97 cm) has an angle of loft on its face of 30°, and the wedge at 36 in (91 cm) has an angle of 52°.

Women's clubs are lighter and slightly shorter than those used by men, and sets are 'fitted' to the players, some requiring lighter or shorter clubs than the standard sizes, or shafts with varying degrees of 'whip'. *(Rule 4–4)*

Waiving the rules

Players must not agree among themselves to waive a rule, local rule or any penalty incurred. *(Rule 1–3)*

General penalty

Except when otherwise provided for, the penalty for the breach of a rule is the loss of a hole in match play or two strokes in stroke play.

Note Certain minor infringements incur a penalty of one stroke. Generally speaking, disqualification occurs only in the case of deliberate infringement. *(Rules 2–6 and 3–5)*

Types of play

Match play In match play, a hole is won by the side which holes its ball in the fewest strokes (after deducting any handicap allowance). The hole is halved if each side holes out in the same number of strokes. A match consists of a stipulated round or rounds, and is won by the side which is leading by a number of holes greater than the number remaining to be played. A player can concede his opponent's next stroke, a hole or the match; this concession may not be declined or withdrawn.

Note Thus, if a side is four up after 15 holes, it has won the match by four up and three to play (usually written as 4 & 3). If, after finishing the 18th hole, each side has won an equal number, the match is halved. If a decision is essential, as in a knock-out tournament or championship, it is usual for the players to begin the round again, the first to win a hole taking the match. Thus a game can be won at the 19th, the 20th and so on. In playing additional holes, handicap strokes are given and taken at the same holes as in the first round. (*Rule 2*)

Stroke play In stroke play, the competitor who completes the stipulated round or rounds in the fewest strokes is the winner.

Note In stroke competitions under handicap, the full handicap allowed the player is deducted from his total, and the net score counts. (*Rule 3*)

Practice during play

During the play of a hole, a player must not play any practice stroke. Between the play of two holes a player cannot play a practice stroke from any hazard, but may practise putting or chipping on or near the putting green of the hole last played, any practice putting green or the teeing ground of the next hole to be played in the ground. On any day of a stroke play competition or play-off, the competitor may not practise on the competition course before a round or play-off. When a competition extends over consecutive days or on different courses, practice on any competition course still to be played between rounds is prohibited.

It is important to note that a practice swing is not a practice stroke, as a stroke is a forward movement of the club with the intention of striking a ball. (*Rule 7*)

Advice and assistance during play

A player may only give advice to, or ask advice from, his partner or either of their caddies. In making a stroke a player must not seek or accept physical assistance or protection from the weather.

A player may have the line of play indicated by anyone (except on the putting green, where only the player's partner or their caddies may do so – the putting green should not be touched in the process). No one can place a mark or stand to indicate the line of play while the stroke is being played.

Note 'Assistance' or 'protection' includes bending back an obstructing bush or shielding a player from wind or rain. (*Rules 8 and 14–2*)

Information as to strokes taken

A player who has incurred a penalty must tell his opponent as soon as possible. The number of strokes a player has taken includes any penalty strokes incurred. A player in match play is entitled at any time during the play of a hole to ask the number of strokes his opponent has taken. If the opponent gives wrong information and fails to correct the mistake before the player has played his next stroke, the opponent loses the hole. (*Rule 9*)

31

Disputes, decisions and doubts as to rights

In match play where there is a dispute about the rules or the number of strokes taken, a claim must be made before the players strike off from the next teeing ground or (in the case of the last hole of the match) before they leave the putting green. Any later claim based on newly discovered facts cannot be considered unless the player making the claim had been given the wrong information by an opponent. In stroke play no penalty may be imposed after the results are posted unless the player knowingly returns a score for a hole lower than actually achieved.

If a referee has been appointed by the Committee, his decision is final. In the absence of a referee, the decision of the Committee is final. If the Committee cannot come to a decision, it refers to the Rules of the Golf Committee of the Royal and Ancient Golf Club of St. Andrews, and its decision is final.

If any point in dispute is not covered by the rules or local rules, the decision is made in accordance with fair play and logic, which is referred to in golf as 'equity'. (*Rule 1–4*)

In stroke play, a competitor who is unsure of his rights or the correct procedure may play out the hole with the original ball and, at the same time, complete the play of the hole with a second ball stating which ball he wishes to score with if that procedure is allowable under the rules. The point is then referred to the Committee for adjudication. If a competitor fails to announce in advance his decision to invoke this rule or state in advance the ball with which he wishes to score, the score with the original ball, rather than the higher score, will count. A player need not report the facts to the Committee if he scores the same with both balls.

These rules do not apply to match play. (*Rules 2–5, 3–3 and 34*)

Order of play on the tee – 'the honour'

A match begins by each side playing a ball from the first teeing ground in order of the draw or by lot. The side which wins a hole takes 'the honour' – plays first at the next teeing ground. In match play an opponent may recall a ball played out of turn, but in stroke play the stroke must stand. In either case there is no penalty. (*Rule 10*)

The teeing ground

The teeing ground is the starting place for the hole to be played. It is a rectangular area two club-lengths in depth, the front and sides of which are defined by the outside limits of two markers. A ball is outside the teeing ground when all of it lies outside the area defined above.

Note   The teeing ground is not necessarily the whole of the flat space prepared for teeing, but only that part in use for the day. The position of the markers is varied from day to day to avoid undue wear and tear of any one particular area. (*Rule 11*)

Playing outside the teeing ground

If a player in a match, when starting a hole, plays a ball from outside the teeing ground there is no penalty, but his opponent may require him to play the stroke again from within the teeing ground. In stroke play, however, he is penalised two strokes and must play the stroke again from the correct place. Strokes played by a competitor from outside the teeing ground do not count in his score. If a competitor fails to rectify his mistake before making a stroke off the next teeing ground, or in the case of the last hole of the round, before leaving the putting green, he is disqualified.

A player may take his stance outside the teeing ground to play a ball within it. (*Rule 11*)

Ball falling off tee

If a ball, when not in play (that is, when a stroke has not yet been made at it) falls off the tee, or is knocked off by the player in addressing it, it may be re-teed without penalty. (*Rule 11–3*)

Order of play in threesome and foursome

In a foursome (two players playing one ball against a similar pair) the partners strike off alternately from the teeing grounds (*A* drives at the first hole and *B* at the second, etc.), and thereafter the partners strike alternately during the play of each hole.

In match play, if a player tees off when his partner should have done, his side loses the hole. The penalty in stroke play is two strokes, or disqualification if the stroke is not rectified by replaying the stroke in the correct order. (*Rule 29*)

Ball played as it lies

The ball should be played as it lies at all times except where the rules or local rules provide otherwise. (*Rule 13–1*)

Improving lie or stance and influencing the ball

Irregularities of surface which could affect a player's lie may not be removed or pressed down by the player, his partner or either of their caddies except: as may occur in fairly taking his stance; in making the stroke or the backward movement of his club for the stroke; when playing from the teeing ground; or repairing old hole plugs or ball marks on the putting green.

If a ball lies in long grass, rushes, bushes, whins, heather or the like, only so much can be touched as will enable the player to find and identify his ball: nothing may be done which can in any way improve its lie.

A player may not improve, or allow to be improved, his line of play, the position or lie of his ball or the area of his intended swing, by bending, moving or breaking anything fixed or growing (except in taking a fair stance to address the ball, and in making the stroke). (*Rules 13–2 and 12–1*)

Loose impediments

A loose impediment may be removed without penalty except when both the impediment and the ball lie in or touch the same hazard. When a ball is moving, a loose impediment on the line of play cannot be removed. (*Rule 23*)

The term 'loose impediments' includes natural objects not fixed or growing and not sticking to the ball, e.g. stones not solidly embedded, leaves, twigs, branches and the like, dung, worms and insects and casts or heaps made by them.

Snow and ice are either casual water or loose impediments, at the option of the player. Dew, however, is not a loose impediment.

Sand and loose soil are loose impediments on the putting green, but not elsewhere on the course.

Striking at the ball

The ball shall be fairly struck with the head of the club, and must not be pushed, scraped or spooned.

If a player, when making a stroke, strikes the ball more than once he counts the stroke and adds a penalty stroke – making two strokes in all. (*Rule 14*)

Ball further from the hole played first

When the balls are in play, the ball furthest from the hole shall be played first. In match play, if a player plays when his opponent should have done so, the opponent may immediately require the player to replay the stroke. In stroke play no penalty is incurred, and the ball should be played as it lies. (*Rule 10*)

Playing a wrong ball or playing from a wrong place

A player must hole out with the ball played from the teeing ground unless he has substituted his ball with another.

Note Generally there is a penalty for playing the wrong ball of two strokes in stroke play or loss of hole in match play. However, if a player in a stroke competition holes out with the wrong ball he is disqualified, unless he rectifies his mistake by finding and holing out with his own ball from the place where the mistake occurred, and provided he has not played a stroke from the next teeing ground. In match play if each side plays the other side's ball and it cannot be settled which side first committed the error, the hole shall be played out with the balls thus exchanged. (*Rule 15*)

There is no penalty for playing a wrong ball from a hazard.

Lifting, dropping, placing, identifying or cleaning ball

Through the green or in a hazard, when a ball is lifted under a rule or local rule or when another ball is to be played, it should be lifted and dropped as near as possible to the spot where the ball lay, except when a rule permits it to be dropped elsewhere or placed. In a hazard a lifted ball must be dropped and come to rest in the hazard; if it rolls out of the hazard it must be re-dropped without penalty. On a putting green the ball should be placed.

A ball may only be dropped by the player himself. He stands erect, holds the ball at shoulder height with outstretched arm and drops it. If a ball is dropped in any other way, the player incurs a penalty stroke unless the error is corrected under *Rule 20–6*. If the ball touches the player before it strikes the ground, the player re-drops without penalty. If the ball touches his partner or either of their caddies or equipment before or after it strikes the ground, the player should proceed correctly, without penalty.

A ball to be lifted under the rules may be lifted by the player or his partner, or by another person authorised by the player. It may be lifted for the purpose of identification but must then be replaced on the same spot.

A ball may be cleaned (except when lifted under rules 5–3, 12–2 and 22) when lifted from an unplayable lie, for relief from an obstruction, from casual water, or ground under repair, from a water hazard, on a wrong green, or on the putting green. (*Rule 21*)

Ball interfering with play

Anywhere on the course a player may have any other ball lifted if he considers that it might interfere with his play or assist the play of another player. A ball so lifted should be replaced after the player has played his stroke. If a ball is accidentally moved when complying with this rule, no penalty is incurred, but the ball so moved should be replaced. (*Rule 22*)

A moving ball

A player may not play while his ball is moving, with the exception of certain cases, e.g. when the ball is moving in water, provided he hits the ball without undue delay, thus not allowing wind or current to better his position. (*Rule 14–6*)

Ball in motion stopped or deflected

If a ball in motion is accidentally stopped or deflected by any outside agency, it is a 'rub of the green' and the ball is played as it lies, without penalty.

If it accidentally lodges in anything moving, the ball is dropped through the green or in a hazard, or placed on the putting green, as near as possible to the spot where the moving object was when the ball lodged in it, without penalty.

If the player's ball in motion is stopped or deflected by him, his partner or either of their caddies, or their clubs or other equipment, the player or his side is penalised two strokes in stroke play or loses the hole in match play. Aside from a stroke played from a putting green, if two balls in motion collide, each player plays his ball as it lies. (*Rule 19*)

Ball at rest moved

If a ball at rest is moved by a fellow competitor or his caddie, or any outside agency, the player replaces the ball, without penalty. If it is impossible to determine the exact spot, the ball is dropped (or placed, in the case of the putting green) as near as possible to the place from which it was moved, and not nearer the hole.

Except while searching for the ball, if it is moved by the opponent in match play the opponent incurs a penalty stroke, and the ball is replaced. If it is moved by the player, whether while searching or not, he incurs a penalty stroke, and the ball is replaced. In stroke play if the ball is moved by a fellow competitor, there is no penalty but the ball must be restored to its original position; but if the ball is moved by the player he incurs a penalty stroke. (*Rule 18*)

Ball unfit for play

If a ball in play is so badly damaged that it becomes unfit for further play, it may be changed by the player after agreeing with his opponent or marker that it is so damaged. Mud on a ball does not make it unfit for play. If a ball breaks into pieces as a result of a stroke, it is replaced with another ball without penalty and the stroke is replayed. (*Rule 5–3*)

Ball lost, out of bounds or unplayable

If a ball is lost outside a water hazard or is out of bounds, the player plays his

next stroke as nearly as possible at the spot from which the original ball was played or moved by him, adding a penalty stroke to his score for the hole. A ball may be declared unplayable at any place on the course except in a water hazard, and the player is the sole judge as to whether his ball is unplayable.

If a player decides his ball is unplayable he either plays his next stroke as provided for a ball lost or out of bounds, i.e. the 'stroke and distance' penalty; or drops a ball, under a penalty of one stroke, either within two club-lengths of the point where the ball lay, but not nearer the hole, or behind the point where the ball lay. In this case he must keep that point between himself and the hole, with no limit to how far behind that point the ball may be dropped. If the ball lay in a bunker, a ball must be dropped in the bunker, if relief is taken in this way. (*Rules 27 and 28*)

Provisional ball

If a ball might be lost outside a water hazard or may be out of bounds, to

save time the player can at once play another ball provisionally, as nearly as possible from the spot at which the original ball was played.

Before playing a provisional ball the player must announce his intention to his opponent or marker, and such a ball may be played only before the player or his partner goes forward to search for the original ball. The player may play a provisional ball until he reaches the place where the original ball is likely to be.

If he plays any strokes with the provisional ball from the point beyond that place, the original ball is deemed to be lost, even if it is later found. If the original ball is lost outside a water hazard or is out of bounds, he continues play with the provisional ball, under penalty of stroke and distance. If the original ball is unplayable in bounds, or lies or is lost in a water hazard, the provisional ball is abandoned. (*Rule 27–2*)

Obstructions

Any movable obstruction may be removed before a shot is played. If the obstruction is immovable, and interferes with the lie of the ball, the player's stance or area of intended swing, except when the ball lies in a water hazard, the ball may be lifted and dropped not more than one club-length away from the point where relief is obtained; such point is determined as the nearest point to where the ball lay where full relief is attained. The ball is dropped, without penalty, and must come to rest not nearer the hole. (*Rule 24*)

If the ball lies in or on a movable obstruction, it may be removed and the ball dropped in the place directly underneath where the ball lay.

Casual water

If a player's ball lies in or touches casual water, ground under repair or a hole, cast or runway made by a burrowing animal, reptile or bird; or if any of these conditions interfere with the player's stance or the area of his intended swing, he may drop a ball (without penalty) on ground which avoids these conditions. It must be within one club-length of the nearest point where the player gets relief.

If a ball lies on the putting green and in casual water, or if casual water intervenes between it and the hole, the ball may be lifted and placed, without penalty, on the nearest spot (not nearer the hole) which will give a clear line to the hole. (*Rule 25*)

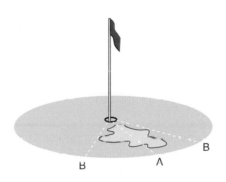

▲ *Fig. 15 If a ball lies on the putting green and casual water intervenes between it and the hole, it may be lifted and placed, without penalty, on the nearest spot (not nearer the hole) which will give a clear line to the hole. In this case, the ball may be moved from A to B*

Hazards and water hazards

When the ball lies in or touches a hazard or water hazard, nothing may be done which can in any way improve its lie. Before making a stroke, the player cannot touch the ground or water with his club, nor touch or move any loose impediments in the hazard.

If the ball lies or is lost in a water hazard, the player can play the ball as it lies, or, under a penalty of one stroke, drop a ball: behind the water hazard, without limit as to distance, keeping the spot at which the ball last crossed the margin of the hazard between himself and the hole; or as near as possible to the spot from which the original ball was played.

A player may drop a ball outside a lateral water hazard within two club-lengths of the margin of either side, opposite the point where the ball last crossed the hazard margin. The ball must come to rest not nearer the hole than this point. (*Rules 13–4 and 26*)

The flagstick

Before or during the stroke, the player may have the flagstick removed or held up at any time to indicate the position of the hole. This may be done only on the authority of the player before he plays his stroke. If the flagstick is attended or removed by an opponent, a fellow competitor or the caddie of either, with the knowledge of the player, and no objection is made, the player is deemed to have authorised it.

If a player's ball strikes the flagstick when it is attended or has been removed, strikes the person standing at the flagstick or equipment carried by him, or strikes an unattended flagstick when played from the putting green, the player incurs a penalty of loss of hole in match play, or two strokes in stroke play.

If the ball is played from off the green and comes to rest against the flagstick when it is in the hole, the player is entitled to have the flagstick removed, and if the ball falls into the hole the player is deemed to have holed out at his last stroke. (*Rule 17*)

The putting green

The line of the putt must not be touched except as provided in the rules, but the player may place the club in front of the ball when addressing it, without pressing anything down. The player may move any loose impediment on the putting green by picking it up or brushing it aside with his hand or a club, without pressing anything down. If the ball is moved, it is replaced without penalty.

The player may repair damage to the putting green caused by the impact of a ball and old hole plugs. The ball may be marked and lifted to permit repair and then replaced on the spot from which it was lifted.

A ball lying on the putting green may be marked and lifted without penalty, cleaned if desired, and replaced on the spot from which it was lifted.

When the ball nearer the hole lies on the putting green, if the player considers it might interfere with his play, he may require the opponent to mark and lift the ball, which must be replaced after the player has played his stroke.

Anyone on the player's side may, before a stroke is made, point out a line for putting, but the following are prohibited: placing a mark on the green; touching the line of the putt in front; testing the surface of the green, rolling a ball on it or roughening or scraping the surface; playing before the other ball is at rest; standing so as to influence the position or movement of the ball; lifting the other ball while the player's ball is in motion.

A ball lying on a putting green other than that of the hole being played must be lifted and dropped off the putting green, not nearer the hole, and within one club length, as near as possible to where the ball lay. There is no penalty. (*Rule 25*)

The player may not make a stroke on the putting green from a stance astride, or with either foot touching, the line of the putt or an extension of the line behind the ball.

If a player putts out of turn during match play, the opponent may require the stroke to be replayed. A ball moved by another ball must be replaced.

In stroke play the ball may be lifted or putted first if the owner considers it might be of assistance to a fellow competitor.

When both balls lie on the green, if the competitor's ball strikes the other he incurs a penalty of two strokes and plays the ball as it lies. The other ball is replaced at once. (*Rules 16 and 19*)

The hole

The 'hole' must be $4^{1}/_{4}$ in (108 mm) in diameter and at least 4 in (100 mm) deep. If a lining is used it should be sunk at least 1 in (25 mm) below the putting green surface, unless the nature of the soil makes it impractical to do so. Its outer diameter should not exceed $4^{1}/_{4}$ in (108 mm).

Readers are strongly advised to read the Rules of Golf in full, but for their information Sections I and II concerning Etiquette and Definitions are reproduced here.

▶ *Fig. 17 A ball lying on the putting green may be marked and lifted without penalty, cleaned if desired, and replaced on the spot from which it was lifted*

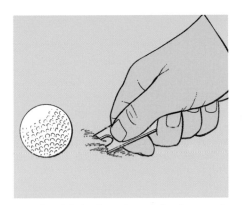

▲ *Fig. 16 A player is permitted to repair damage to the putting green caused by the impact of a ball*

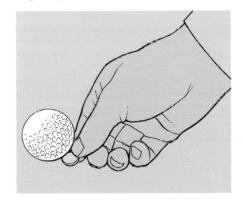

39

Etiquette

Courtesy on the course

Safety   Prior to playing a stroke or making a practice swing, the player should ensure that no one is standing close by or in a position to be hit by the club, the ball or any stones, pebbles, twigs or the like which may be moved by the stroke or swing.

Consideration for other players   The player who has the honour should be allowed to play before his opponent or fellow competitor tees his ball.

No one should move, talk or stand close to or directly behind the ball or the hole when a player is addressing the ball or making a stroke.

In the interest of all, players should play without delay.

No player should play until the players in front are out of range.

Players searching for a ball should signal the players behind them to pass as soon as it becomes apparent that the ball will not easily be found. They should not search for five minutes before doing so. They should not continue play until the players following them have passed and are out of range.

When the play of a hole has been completed, players should immediately leave the putting green.

Priority on the course

In the absence of special rules, two-ball matches should have precedence over and be entitled to pass any three- or four-ball match.

A single player has no standing and should give way to a match of any kind.

Any match playing a whole round is entitled to pass a match playing a shorter round.

If a match fails to keep its place on the course and loses more than one clear hole on the players in front, it should invite the match following to pass.

Care of the course

Holes in bunkers   Before leaving a bunker, a player should carefully fill up and smooth over all holes and footprints made by him.

Replace divots; repair ball-marks and damage by spikes   Through the green, a player should ensure that any turf cut or displaced by him is replaced at once and pressed down and that any damage to the putting green made by a ball is carefully repaired. Damage to the putting green caused by golf shoe spikes should be repaired *on completion of the hole.*

Damage to greens – flagsticks, bags, etc. Players should ensure that, when putting down bags or the flagstick, no damage is done to the putting green and that neither they nor their caddies damage the hole by standing close to it, in handling the flagstick or in removing the ball from the hole. The flagstick should be properly replaced in the hole before the players leave the putting green. Players should not damage the putting green by leaning on their putters, particularly when removing the ball from the hole.

Golf carts Local notices regulating the movement of golf carts should be strictly observed.

Damage from practice swings In taking practice swings, players should avoid causing damage to the course, particularly the tees, by removing divots.

Definitions

Addressing the ball

A player has 'addressed the ball' when he has taken his stance and has also grounded his club, except that in a hazard a player has addressed the ball when he has taken his stance.

Advice

'Advice' is any counsel or suggestion which could influence a player in determining his play, the choice of a club, or the method of making a stroke.

Information on the rules or local rules, or on matters of public information such as the position of hazards or the flagstick on the putting green, is not advice.

Ball moved

A ball is deemed to have 'moved' if it leaves its position and comes to rest in any other place.

Ball in play, provisional ball, wrong ball

• A ball is 'in play' as soon as the player has made a stroke on the teeing ground. It remains as his ball in play until holed out, except when it is out of bounds, lost or lifted, or another ball has been substituted under an applicable rule or local rule: a ball so substituted becomes the ball in play.

• A 'provisional ball' is a ball played under rule 27–2 for a ball which may be lost outside a water hazard or may be out of bounds.

• A 'wrong ball' is any ball other than the ball in play or a provisional ball or, in stroke play, a second ball in accordance with rule 3–3 or 20–7b.

Ball lost

A ball is 'lost' if:

• it is not found, or is not identified as his by the player, within five minutes after the player's side or his or their caddies have begun to search for it; or
• the player has put another ball into play under the rules, even though he may not have searched for the original ball; or
• the player has played any stroke with a provisional ball from a point nearer the hole than the place where the original ball is likely to be, whereupon the provisional ball becomes the ball in play.

Time spent in playing a wrong ball is not counted in the five-minute period allowed for the search.

Caddie

A 'caddie' is one who carries or handles a player's clubs during play and otherwise assists him in accordance with the rules. A player may have only one caddie at any one time.

When one caddie is employed by more than one player, he is always deemed to be the caddie of the player whose ball is involved, and equipment carried by him is deemed to be that player's equipment, except when the caddie acts upon specific directions from another player, in which case he is considered to be that other player's caddie.

Committee

The 'Committee' is the committee in charge of the competition, or, if the matter does not arise in a competition, the committee in charge of the course.

Casual water

'Casual water' is any temporary accumulation of water which is visible before or after the player takes his stance and which is not in a water hazard. Snow and ice are either casual water or loose impediments, at the option of the player. Dew is not casual water.

Competitor

A 'competitor' is a player in a stroke competition. A 'fellow competitor' is any person with whom he plays. Neither is partner of the other. In stroke play foursome and four-ball competitions, where the context so admits, the word 'competitor' or 'fellow competitor' shall be held to include his partner.

Course

The 'course' is the whole area within which play is permitted. (*Rule 33–2*)

Equipment

'Equipment' is anything used, worn or carried by or for the player except any ball he has played and any small object, such as a coin or a tee, when used to mark the position of a ball or the extent of an area in which a ball is to be dropped. Equipment includes a golf cart, whether or not motorised. If such a cart is shared by more than one player, its status under the rules is the same as that of a caddie employed by more than one player. *See* 'Caddie'.

Flagstick

The 'flagstick' is a movable straight indicator with or without bunting or other material attached, centred in the hole to show its position. It shall be circular in cross-section.

Forecaddie

A 'forecaddie' is one who is employed by the Committee to indicate to players the position of balls on the course, and is an 'outside agency'.

Ground under repair

'Ground under repair' is any portion of the course so marked by order of the Committee or its authorised representative. It includes material piled for removal and a hole made by a greenkeeper, even if not so marked. Stakes and lines defining ground under repair are in such ground.

All ground and any grass, bush, tree or other growing thing within the ground under repair is part of the ground under repair. The margin of the ground under repair extends vertically downwards, but not upwards.

Note 1 Grass cuttings and other material left on the course which have been abandoned and are not intended to be removed are not ground under repair unless so marked.

Note 2 The Committee may make a local rule prohibiting play from ground under repair.

Hazards

A 'hazard' is any bunker or water hazard.

Hole

The 'hole' shall be 4¼ in (108 mm) in diameter and at least 4 in (100 mm) deep. If a lining is used, it shall be sunk at least 1 in (25 mm) below the putting green surface unless the nature of the soil makes it impractica-ble to do so: its outer diameter shall not exceed 4¼ in (108 mm).

Holed

A ball is 'holed' when it lies within the circumference of the hole and all of it is below the level of the lip of the hole.

Honour

The side which is entitled to play first from the teeing ground is said to have the 'honour'.

Lateral water hazard

A 'lateral water hazard' is a water hazard or that part of a water hazard so situated that it is not possible, or is deemed by the Committee to be impracticable, to drop a ball behind and keep the spot at which the ball last crossed the hazard margin between player and hole. That part of the water hazard to be played as a lateral water hazard should be distinctively marked.

Note Lateral water hazards should be defined by red stakes or lines.

Line of play

The 'line of play' is the direction which the player wishes his ball to take after a stroke, plus a reasonable distance on either side of the intended direction. The line of play extends vertically upwards from the ground, but does not extend beyond the hole.

Line of putt

The 'line of putt' is the line which the player wishes his ball to take after a stroke on the *putting green*. Except with respect to rule 16–1e, the line of putt includes a reasonable distance on either side of the intended line. The line of putt does not extend beyond the hole.

Loose impediments

The term 'loose impediments' denotes natural objects not fixed or growing and not adhering to the ball, and includes stones not solidly embedded, leaves, twigs, branches and the like, dung, worms and insects, and casts or heaps made by them. Snow and ice are either casual water or loose impediments, at the option of the player.

Sand and loose soil are loose impediments on the putting green, but not elsewhere on the course.

Marker

A 'marker' is a scorer in stroke play who is appointed by the Committee to record a competitor's score. He may be a fellow competitor. He is not a referee.

Observer

An 'observer' is appointed by the Committee to assist a referee to decide questions of fact and to report to him any breach of a rule or local rule. An observer should not attend the flagstick, stand at or mark the position of the hole, or lift the ball or mark its position.

Obstructions

An 'obstruction' is anything artificial, including artificial surfaces and sides of roads and paths, and manufactured ice, except:

- objects defining out of bounds, such as walls, fences, stakes and railings
- any part of an immovable artificial object which is out of bounds
- any construction declared by the Committee to be an integral part of the course.

Out of bounds

'Out of bounds' is beyond the boundaries of the course or any part of the course so marked by the committee.

When out of bounds is defined by reference to stakes or a fence, the out of bounds line is determined by the nearest inside points of the stakes or fence posts at ground level excluding angled supports. When out of bounds is fixed by a line on the ground the line itself is out of bounds.

A ball is out of bounds when all of it lies out of bounds.

The out of bounds line is deemed to extend vertically upwards and downwards.

The player may stand out of bounds to play a ball lying within bounds.

Outside agency

An 'outside agency' is any agency not part of the match or, in stroke play, not part of a competitor's side, and includes a referee, a marker, an observer, or a forecaddie.

Neither wind nor water is an outside agency.

Partner

A 'partner' is a player associated with another player on the same side. In a threesome, foursome, or a four-ball where the context so admits, the word 'player' shall be held to include his partner.

Penalty stroke

A 'penalty stroke' is one added to the score of a side under certain rules. In a threesome or foursome, penalty strokes do not affect the order of play.

Provisional ball

A 'provisional ball' is a ball played under rule 27–2 for a ball which may be lost outside a water hazard or may be out of bounds.

Putting green

The 'putting green' is all ground of the hole being played which is specially prepared for putting or otherwise defined as such by the Committee.

A ball is deemed to be on the putting green when any part of it touches the putting green.

Referee

A 'referee' is one who is appointed by the Committee to accompany the players to decide questions of fact and apply the Rules of Golf. He shall act on any breach of rule or local rule which he may observe or which may be reported to him.

A referee should not attend the flagstick, stand at or mark the position of the hole or lift the ball or mark its position.

Rub of the green

A 'rub of the green' occurs when a ball in motion is stopped or deflected by any outside agency. (*Rule 19–1*)

Sides and matches

Side:	a player or two or more players who are partners.
Single:	a match in which one plays against another.
Threesome:	a match in which one plays against two, and each side plays one ball.
Foursome:	a match in which two play against two, and each side plays one ball.
Three-ball:	a match in which three play against one another, each playing his own ball.

	Each player is play-
	ing two distinct
	matches.
Best-ball:	a match in which
	one plays against the
	better ball of two or
	the best ball of three
	players.
Four-ball:	a match in which
	two play their better
	ball against the
	better ball of two
	other players.

Note In a best-ball or four-ball match, if a partner is absent for reasons satisfactory to the Committee, the remaining member(s) of his side may represent the side.

Stance

Taking the 'stance' consists of a player placing his feet in position for and preparatory to making a stroke.

Stipulated round

The 'stipulated round' consists of playing the holes of the course in their correct sequence unless otherwise authorised by the Committee. The number of holes in a stipulated round is 18 unless a smaller number is authorised by the Committee.

As to extension of stipulated round in match play, see *Rule 2–3*.

Stroke

A 'stroke' is the forward movement of the club made with the intention of fairly striking at and moving the ball. If a player checks his down-swing voluntarily before the club-head reaches the ball, he is deemed not to have made a stroke.

Teeing ground

The 'teeing ground' is the starting place for the hole to be played. It is a rectangular area two club-lengths in depth, the front and the sides of which are defined by the outside limits of two tee markers. A ball is outside the teeing ground when all of it lies outside the teeing ground.

Through the green

'Through the green' is the whole area of the course except:

● the teeing ground and putting green of the hole being played
● all hazards on the course.

Water hazard

A 'water hazard' is any sea, lake, pond, river, ditch, surface drainage ditch or other open water course (whether or not containing water) and anything of a similar nature.

All ground or water within the margin of a water hazard is part of the water hazard. The margin of a water hazard is deemed to extend vertically upwards. Stakes and lines defining the margins of water hazards are in the hazard.

Note Water hazards (other than lateral water hazards) should be defined by yellow stakes or lines.

Wrong ball

A 'wrong ball' is any ball other than the player's:

- ball in play
- provisional ball, or
- (in stroke play) second ball played under rule 3–3 or rule 20–7b

Note Ball in play includes a ball substituted for the ball in play whether or not substitution is permitted.

The Professional Golfers' Association

The Professional Golfers' Association (PGA) is a members' organisation of approximately 3,000 qualified golf professionals, who between them employ nearly 1,000 registered trainees. The PGA is dedicated to training and serving golf professionals, whose main aim is to offer a highly efficient service to amateur golfers at clubs, driving ranges and other golf establishments.

The objectives of the PGA are to promote interest in the game of golf; to protect and advance the mutual and trade interests of its members; to arrange and hold meetings and tournaments for members; to operate a benevolent fund for the relief of deserving members; to assist members in obtaining employment, and to effect any other objectives determined by the Association.

For further information on the PGA and its work, please write to: The PGA, Centenary House, The Belfry, Sutton Coldfield, West Midlands, B76 9PT.

Index